We Believe

COMPANION JOURNAL

Copyright © 2026 by Gary Lewis

Published by Arrows & Stones

All rights reserved. No portion of this book may be reproduced, stored in a retrieval system, or transmitted in any form or by any means—electronic, mechanical, photocopy, recording, scanning, or other—except for brief quotations in critical reviews or articles, without prior written permission of the author.

For foreign and subsidiary rights, contact the author.

Cover design by: Sara Young

ISBN: 978-1-969062-12-4   1 2 3 4 5 6 7 8 9 10

Printed in the United States of America

FEBRUARY

COMPANION JOURNAL

We Believe

A Journey of Faith in Action

GARY LEWIS

CONTENTS

How S.O.A.P Works ix

DAY 32. **February 1** 10

DAY 33. **February 2** 14

DAY 34. **February 3** 17

DAY 35. **February 4** 20

DAY 36. **February 5** 23

DAY 37. **February 6** 26

DAY 38. **February 7** 29

DAY 39. **February 8** 32

DAY 40. **February 9** 35

DAY 41. **February 10** 38

DAY 42. **February 11** 41

DAY 43. **February 12** 44

DAY 44. **February 13** 47

DAY 45. **February 14** 50

DAY 46. **February 15** 53

DAY 47. **February 16** 56

DAY 48. **February 17** 59

DAY 49. **February 18** 62

DAY 50. **February 19** 65

DAY 51. **February 20** 68

DAY 52. **February 21** 71

DAY 53. **February 22** 74

DAY 54. **February 23** 77

DAY 55. **February 24** 80

DAY 56. **February 25** 83

DAY 57. **February 26** 86

DAY 58. **February 27** 89

DAY 59. **February 28** 92

HOW S.O.A.P WORKS

Each day, you will complete a set of prompts using the S.O.A.P. method. S.O.A.P. is a simple way to deepen your time in God's Word.

Start with **Scripture**. Read a passage relevant to the main theme of the day's readings and, if possible, write it down to engage with it more fully.

Next, move to **Observation**: consider what stands out to you in that passage. Is there something in the main message—a word, a phrase, or thought that resonates with you?

Then, shift to **Application**. Ask God how He wants you to apply this truth in your life.

Finally, end with **Prayer**. Lift your needs and pray for others as you invite God to work in your heart through His Word.

FEBRUARY 1

DAY 32 OF 365

DEVOTIONAL

A new month is another reminder of God's faithfulness. Time itself is a gift, and each new beginning invites us to look again at who God is and what it means to believe Him. The book of Job pulls us straight into the tension of faith. In Job 22-24, his friends insist he must have sinned, but Job pleads for an audience with God. He cannot reconcile his suffering with the prosperity of the wicked, yet he continues to cry out. Faith does not pretend to have all the answers; it dares to bring honest questions before the Lord, believing that He alone is righteous and just.

That same call to genuine faith rises in Matthew 21:18-32. Jesus curses a fig tree that bore leaves but no fruit, showing that appearance without substance is empty. Then He tells a parable of two sons—one who said "yes" but disobeyed, and one who said "no" yet ultimately did his father's will. In both pictures, belief is not measured by outward show but by obedience to God's Word. The Spirit presses this truth deeper: genuine faith bears fruit in action.

Proverbs 3:21-35 ties these threads together, urging us to hold fast to wisdom. God's wisdom brings life and peace, protecting us from envy and from the path of the wicked. When Job longed for justice and when Jesus warned against empty religion, both pointed to this truth: trusting God's wisdom is the way to life.

As we step into February, let these passages remind us that belief is not about appearances, quick answers, or empty words. It is about trusting the God who hears, obeying the voice of Christ, and leaning on the Spirit to guide us into wisdom. His justice will prevail, and His promises will stand.

Pray with me:
"Lord, thank You for the gift of a new month. Help me walk in wisdom, not empty words. Shape my faith so it bears real fruit. When I face questions without easy answers, remind me that You are just and faithful. I choose to believe Your Word and trust Your Spirit to guide me."

TODAY'S READINGS

JOB 22   JOB 23   JOB 24
MATTHEW 21:18-32   PROVERBS 3:21-35

S.O.A.P

SCRIPTURE

OBSERVATION

APPLICATION

PRAYER

FEBRUARY 2
DAY 33 OF 365

DEVOTIONAL

In Job 25-29, Job's friends offer shallow answers, but Job speaks of God's unmatched power and the priceless value of wisdom. True understanding, he says, belongs to God alone. Faith learns to trust the Spirit's wisdom rather than leaning on human opinion.

Jesus echoes this in Matthew 21:33-46 and 22:1-14. He warns that rejecting God's call has eternal weight, but those who believe and respond are welcomed into His kingdom. Job's longing for wisdom finds its fulfillment in Christ, who is the cornerstone of God's plan.

Psalm 18:7-15 reminds us that this God of wisdom is also a God of power, shaking the earth and thundering from heaven to deliver His people. His wisdom and might are always working together for our good.

Today, ask the Spirit to clothe you with God's wisdom, so your life responds faithfully to His call.

TODAY'S READINGS

JOB 25   JOB 26   JOB 27   JOB 28   JOB 29
MATTHEW 21:33-46   MATTHEW 22:1-14   PSALM 18:7-15

…

S.O.A.P

SCRIPTURE

OBSERVATION

APPLICATION

PRAYER

FEBRUARY 3
DAY 34 OF 365

DEVOTIONAL

In Job 30-32, Job laments his suffering while Elihu begins to speak of God's justice. Job's cries remind us how deeply we long for deliverance when life feels unfair.

Jesus shows that deliverance is found in love and truth.

In Matthew 22:15-46, He silences His challengers and declares the greatest commandment: to love God and love others. Just as Job longed for rescue, Christ reveals that obedience and love are the fruit of true belief, and we believe this way of love is the path of freedom.

Psalm 18:16-24 confirms it: God rescues the faithful, drawing them out of deep waters and setting their feet on solid ground. We believe His deliverance is not only for yesterday but also for today.

Today, ask the Spirit to anchor your confidence in God's deliverance, even when the path feels uncertain.

TODAY'S READINGS

JOB 30   JOB 31   JOB 32   MATTHEW 22:15-46   PSALM 18:16-24

S.O.A.P

SCRIPTURE

OBSERVATION

APPLICATION

PRAYER

FEBRUARY 4

DAY 35 OF 365

DEVOTIONAL

In Job 33-34, Elihu reminds Job that God speaks through suffering and always acts justly. He insists that the Almighty cannot do wrong, pressing Job to see that God's wisdom is higher than ours. Even when answers are hidden, we believe His purposes are sure.

In Matthew 23, Jesus condemns the hypocrisy of the Pharisees, showing that God's justice cannot be fooled by appearances. Both Elihu's warning and Christ's rebuke remind us that God sees the heart and calls His people to live with sincerity. We must know that His justice is both searching and fair, exposing what is false and affirming what is true.

Psalm 18:25-36 celebrates this justice, declaring that God shows Himself faithful to the faithful and blameless to the blameless. His ways are perfect, and His strength equips us to walk uprightly.

Today, let the Spirit form integrity in you, so your life reflects God's justice and truth.

TODAY'S READINGS

JOB 33   JOB 34   MATTHEW 23   PSALM 18:25-36

S.O.A.P

SCRIPTURE

OBSERVATION

APPLICATION

PRAYER

FEBRUARY 5
DAY 36 OF 365

DEVOTIONAL

Job 35-37 lifts our eyes to God's greatness, whose wisdom is beyond human grasp. Elihu's words remind us that storms, thunder, and creation itself testify to His majesty. Faith means believing the Spirit knows what we cannot, and that His wisdom guides us when ours fails.

In Matthew 24:1-31, Jesus speaks of the end times, urging His disciples not to be deceived but to endure in faith. Just as Job was called to trust what he could not understand, God's wisdom will carry us through every trial. Even when uncertainty rises, His Word stands secure, pointing us to His eternal kingdom.

Proverbs 4:1-9 teaches that wisdom is worth more than riches and is a crown of glory to those who embrace it. The Lord gives wisdom freely to His people, and He delights to guide those who seek Him.

Today, ask the Spirit for wisdom, trusting Him to anchor your heart in every season.

TODAY'S READINGS

JOB 35   JOB 36   JOB 37   MATTHEW 24:1-31   PROVERBS 4:1-9

WE BELIEVE

S.O.A.P

SCRIPTURE

OBSERVATION

APPLICATION

PRAYER

FEBRUARY 6
DAY 37 OF 365

DEVOTIONAL

In Job 38-40:2, God answers Job out of the storm, reminding him of His power in creation. Job's doubts are quieted, not by explanation, but by a vision of God's greatness. We must believe that faith rests secure when fixed on His majesty.

In Matthew 24:32-51 and 25:1-13, Jesus calls His followers to stay awake and ready for His return. Just as Job learned awe before God, we are called to live expectantly, trusting that the kingdom will come in God's timing. Belief shapes how we wait—watchful, faithful, and filled with the Spirit's oil.

Psalm 18:37-42 reminds us that God gives victory to His people, strengthening them to overcome. His kingdom belongs to the Lord, who reigns forever.

Today, let the Spirit awaken expectancy in you, shaping your life in readiness for Christ's return.

TODAY'S READINGS

JOB 38   JOB 39   JOB 40:1-2
MATTHEW 24:32-51   MATTHEW 25:1-13   PSALM 18:37-42

S.O.A.P

SCRIPTURE

OBSERVATION

APPLICATION

PRAYER

FEBRUARY 7
DAY 38 OF 365

DEVOTIONAL

In Job 40-42, Job humbles himself before God's greatness as the Lord reminds him of His unmatched power over creation, even Leviathan. Job repents, and God restores what was lost, doubling his blessings and granting peace. What seemed like defeat becomes victory, showing that surrender is the doorway to restoration and new life.

In Matthew 25:14-46, Jesus teaches that true faith is revealed in faithful stewardship and compassionate love. Job's restoration and Christ's parable both point us to the truth that God's victory is not just personal—it overflows into others' lives through obedience.

Psalm 18:43-50 celebrates the Lord who delivers His people and shows steadfast love to His anointed. His victory is sure, His love never fails, and His triumph calls us to live faithfully under His reign.

Today, thank the Spirit for God's victory in your life and live as a faithful servant of His kingdom.

TODAY'S READINGS

JOB 40:3-24   JOB 41   JOB 42
MATTHEW 25:14-46   PSALM 18:43-50

S.O.A.P

SCRIPTURE

OBSERVATION

APPLICATION

PRAYER

FEBRUARY 8
DAY 39 OF 365

DEVOTIONAL

Exodus 1-3 shows Israel suffering in Egypt until God raises up Moses. From the burning bush, He calls Moses into a mission that feels impossible, yet promises to be with him at every step. God equips those He calls and provides the strength they lack.

In Matthew 26:1-30, Jesus reveals His greater calling as the true Passover Lamb, offering His body and blood for the salvation of the world. Just as Moses was sent to deliver Israel, Christ steps into His calling to redeem all people, showing us that God's call always leads to life and freedom.

Psalm 19:1-6 reminds us that creation itself proclaims God's glory, testifying that His call echoes across the earth. We believe His invitation still goes out today, drawing hearts to trust Him.

Today, trust the Spirit to empower you to walk boldly in the call God has placed on your life.

TODAY'S READINGS

EXODUS 1   EXODUS 2   EXODUS 3
MATTHEW 26:1-30   PSALM 19:1-6

S.O.A.P

SCRIPTURE

OBSERVATION

APPLICATION

PRAYER

FEBRUARY 9
DAY 40 OF 365

DEVOTIONAL

In Exodus 4-6:12, Moses doubts his ability, and Pharaoh resists God's command, yet the Lord promises His power will prevail. God reminds Moses that deliverance doesn't rest on human strength but on His mighty hand. It's clear that His strength is made perfect in our weakness.

In Matthew 26:31-46, Jesus prays in Gethsemane, surrendering to the Father's will in deep anguish. Where Moses wavered, Christ showed perfect obedience, teaching us that true power is found in surrender. The Spirit shows us that victory often comes through trust rather than striving.

Proverbs 4:10-19 urges us to walk in wisdom, shining like the light of dawn. The Spirit gives us power to endure and stay the course, leading us away from darkness and into the way of life.

Today, lean on the Spirit's power to overcome fear and walk in God's will.

TODAY'S READINGS

EXODUS 4   EXODUS 5   EXODUS 6:1-12
MATTHEW 26:31-46   PROVERBS 4:10-19

S.O.A.P

SCRIPTURE

OBSERVATION

APPLICATION

PRAYER

FEBRUARY 10
DAY 41 OF 365

DEVOTIONAL

Exodus 6:13-30 through Exodus 8 reveals God's authority over Pharaoh through miraculous signs and plagues. Each act was not only a judgment on Egypt but also a declaration that the Lord alone is God. The strongest ruler on earth could not withstand Him because His authority still reigns over every power and every nation.

In Matthew 26:47-68, Jesus is betrayed and arrested, yet declares that all authority is His. Even in apparent weakness, His kingdom cannot be shaken, for His rule does not rest on human power but on the eternal purposes of God. What looked like defeat was in fact the triumph of obedience and faith.

Psalm 19:7-14 celebrates God's law as perfect, trustworthy, and true. His authority brings life, keeps us pure, and equips us to live in the light of His truth. To submit to God's Word is to find freedom and strength.

Today, ask the Spirit to deepen your trust in God's authority, even when opposition rises.

TODAY'S READINGS

EXODUS 6:13-30   EXODUS 7   EXODUS 8
MATTHEW 26:47-68   PSALM 19:7-14

S.O.A.P

SCRIPTURE

OBSERVATION

APPLICATION

PRAYER

FEBRUARY 11
DAY 42 OF 365

DEVOTIONAL

Exodus 9-10 reveals plague after plague striking Egypt, each proving the Lord's sovereignty over creation and kingdoms. Pharaoh's heart remained hard, but God's purposes could not be stopped. His sovereignty rules over every circumstance, even when leaders resist Him or when our prayers seem delayed.

In Matthew 26:69-75 and 27:1-10, Peter denies Jesus and Judas despairs, yet the plan of redemption presses forward. Human weakness and betrayal could not derail the cross. What looked like failure was still under God's control, reminding us that His sovereignty is greater than our shortcomings.

Psalm 20 reminds us that while some trust in chariots and horses, we believe in the name of the Lord our God. His sovereignty is our confidence, and His name is our refuge.

Today, rest in the Spirit's assurance that God's sovereignty holds your life steady, even in moments of fear or failure.

TODAY'S READINGS

EXODUS 9   EXODUS 10   MATTHEW 26:69-75
MATTHEW 27:1-10   PSALM 20

S.O.A.P

SCRIPTURE

OBSERVATION

APPLICATION

PRAYER

FEBRUARY 12
DAY 43 OF 365

DEVOTIONAL

Exodus 11-12 describes the first Passover, when Israel trusted God's words and found safety under the blood of the lamb. Their deliverance was not earned but received through obedience and belief, and just like then, God still delivers His people today when they trust His promise, covering them with mercy.

In Matthew 27:11-44, Jesus becomes the true Passover Lamb, shedding His blood for the salvation of the world. What was foreshadowed in Egypt is fulfilled at the cross, where the greatest deliverance of all took place. Our faith rests in the Lamb who died in our place.

Psalm 21:1-7 rejoices in the Lord's strength and salvation. We believe His deliverance is complete in Christ and continues to sustain us day by day.

Today, give thanks to the Spirit for the Lamb who has delivered you from sin and death.

TODAY'S READINGS

EXODUS 11   EXODUS 12
MATTHEW 27:11-44   PSALM 21:1-7

S.O.A.P

SCRIPTURE

OBSERVATION

APPLICATION

PRAYER

FEBRUARY 13
DAY 44 OF 365

DEVOTIONAL

Exodus 13-14 shows God leading His people out of bondage and parting the sea before them. What looked like certain death became salvation by His hand. He is still the God who makes a way where there is none, turning obstacles into testimonies and fear into songs of praise.

In Matthew 27:45-66, Jesus dies and is buried, and darkness seems to triumph. Yet even in the silence of the tomb, God's salvation was being accomplished. Hope was hidden, but it was not gone—for the story was not over.

Proverbs 4:20-27 urges us to guard our hearts and fix our eyes ahead. We believe salvation calls us to walk with focus, holiness, and faith, trusting that His Word lights our way and keeps our steps secure.

Today, let the Spirit steady your heart in the salvation Christ has secured for you.

TODAY'S READINGS

EXODUS 13 **EXODUS 14**
MATTHEW 27:45-66 **PROVERBS 4:20-27**

S.O.A.P

SCRIPTURE

OBSERVATION

APPLICATION

PRAYER

FEBRUARY 14
DAY 45 OF 365

DEVOTIONAL

Exodus 15-16 reveals God providing water and manna in the wilderness, teaching His people to depend daily on Him. They discovered that provision is received in faith, reminding us that trust is renewed each morning. His provision never fails, and He delights to meet the needs of His children.

In Matthew 28, the risen Jesus provides something greater than food or water—new life and the promise of His presence to the end of the age. The resurrection is God's ultimate provision, satisfying every need. His presence is the bread that never runs out, and His Spirit is the well that never runs dry.

Psalm 21:8-13 celebrates God's strength and victory over His enemies. We believe His provision gives us both strength for today and confidence for tomorrow, securing our hope in every season.

Today, trust the Spirit to supply all you need and rejoice in the risen Christ who is always with you.

TODAY'S READINGS

EXODUS 15   EXODUS 16
MATTHEW 28   PSALM 21:8-13

S.O.A.P

SCRIPTURE

OBSERVATION

APPLICATION

PRAYER

FEBRUARY 15

DAY 46 OF 365

DEVOTIONAL

In Exodus 17-18, God provides water from the rock and wisdom through Jethro's counsel, showing His presence in both provision and leadership. His presence sustains His people in the wilderness and gives direction when burdens feel overwhelming. He is near in every challenge, guiding us with wisdom and grace.

In Mark 1:1-28, Jesus proclaims the good news, calls disciples, and drives out evil spirits. His ministry reveals that God's presence has come near in power and authority, and it still does through the Spirit today. Wherever the kingdom is proclaimed, His presence breaks through with freedom.

Psalm 22:1-11 captures the cry of one who feels forsaken yet clings to God's presence. We believe He is with us, even in the moments when He feels far away, and His nearness is our hope and security.

Today, ask the Spirit to make you more aware of God's presence, bringing strength and hope wherever you are.

TODAY'S READINGS

EXODUS 17   EXODUS 18
MARK 1:1-28   PSALM 22:1-11

S.O.A.P

SCRIPTURE

OBSERVATION

APPLICATION

PRAYER

FEBRUARY 16
DAY 47 OF 365

DEVOTIONAL

Exodus 19-20 shows God descending on Sinai in fire and cloud, giving His law to guide His people. His holiness reveals both His greatness and His mercy, reminding Israel that they belonged to Him alone.

In Mark 1:29-45, Jesus heals the sick and cleanses the leper, showing that God's power to save reaches into body and soul. In Mark 2:1-17, He forgives sins and calls sinners to follow, proving that His saving power restores what is broken. The same God who thundered on Sinai stoops in compassion through Christ.

Psalm 22:12-21 cries out for rescue in weakness. God's power to save is near to all who call on Him, whether from the mountain or the valley, and His strength is enough to carry us through.

Today, invite the Spirit to write God's truth on your heart and to make His saving power known through you.

TODAY'S READINGS

EXODUS 19   EXODUS 20
MARK 1:29-45   MARK 2:1-17   PSALM 22:12-21

S.O.A.P

SCRIPTURE

OBSERVATION

APPLICATION

PRAYER

FEBRUARY 17
DAY 48 OF 365

DEVOTIONAL

Exodus 21-22 sets out laws for Israel's life together, showing God's care for justice and His concern for the vulnerable. These instructions revealed that belonging to God meant living differently, shaped by His character and marked by compassion toward others.

Jesus expands this vision in Mark 2:18-28 and 3:1-30, teaching that mercy matters more than ritual and that the kingdom stands in the power of the Spirit. His actions confronted hardened hearts, proving that belief is shown not by appearances but by surrender to God's rule, where love fulfills the law.

Proverbs 5:1-14 warns of paths that lead to ruin. Choosing God's way is not restriction but freedom—the path where justice and mercy walk hand in hand and where faith is lived out in everyday choices.

Today, ask the Spirit to align your steps with God's ways, so your life bears witness to His mercy and justice.

TODAY'S READINGS

EXODUS 21   EXODUS 22
MARK 2:18-28   MARK 3:1-30   PROVERBS 5:1-14

S.O.A.P

SCRIPTURE

OBSERVATION

APPLICATION

PRAYER

FEBRUARY 18
DAY 49 OF 365

DEVOTIONAL

Exodus 23-24 shows God confirming His covenant with Israel in blood and glory, inviting His people to walk in His promises. Their obedience was to be an expression of trust, rooted in His presence and shaped by His faithfulness through every generation.

In Mark 3:31-35 and 4:1-29, Jesus redefines family as those who do God's will and describes the kingdom like seed—hidden, growing, and fruitful in believing hearts. His words remind us that covenant life is not about status but about listening and responding, trusting that unseen growth will one day yield a harvest.

Psalm 22:22-31 erupts with praise: "All the ends of the earth will remember and turn to the Lord." Faith clings to this vision, confident that God's Word never returns empty but always accomplishes His purpose.

Today, let the Spirit plant His Word deep within you, so it bears fruit for His kingdom.

TODAY'S READINGS

EXODUS 23   EXODUS 24
MARK 3:31-35   MARK 4:1-29   PSALM 22:22-31

S.O.A.P

SCRIPTURE

OBSERVATION

APPLICATION

PRAYER

FEBRUARY 19

DAY 50 OF 365

DEVOTIONAL

Exodus 25-26 details the tabernacle, where God chose to dwell with His people. Every instruction for its design pointed to His presence as the true center of their life and worship, reminding them that He was both holy and near.

In Mark 4:30-41 and 5:1-20, Jesus speaks of mustard-seed faith, stills the storm, and frees the oppressed. Just as the tabernacle signaled God's nearness in Israel's midst, Christ shows that His presence brings peace in chaos and freedom where fear reigns. The same God who dwelt among His people now demonstrates His authority over creation and the powers of darkness.

Psalm 23 assures us that the Lord is our shepherd, leading us through valleys and into rest. Belief is not wishful thinking but steady trust in the One who walks with us.

Today, invite the Spirit to calm your fears and remind you that Christ is present in every storm.

TODAY'S READINGS

EXODUS 25   EXODUS 26
MARK 4:30-41   MARK 5:1-20   PSALM 23

S.O.A.P

SCRIPTURE

OBSERVATION

APPLICATION

PRAYER

FEBRUARY 20
DAY 51 OF 365

DEVOTIONAL

Exodus 27-28 describes altars and priestly garments, preparing a people to draw near to a holy God. Access to Him was possible only through sacrifice and mediation, reminders that holiness required both cleansing and covering.

Mark 5:21-43 and 6:1-6 show Jesus embodying this access—raising the dead, healing the broken, and honoring faith where others mocked. The holiness once veiled in garments now flows freely through Christ, who welcomes the desperate and meets them with power. His presence restores what no ritual could accomplish on its own.

Psalm 24 declares, "Who may ascend the hill of the Lord? He who has clean hands and a pure heart." Belief clings not to our worthiness but to the One who makes us clean, granting us confidence to stand in God's presence.

Today, let the Spirit remind you that Christ has opened the way for restoration and life.

TODAY'S READINGS

EXODUS 27   EXODUS 28
MARK 5:21-43   MARK 6:1-6   PSALM 24

S.O.A.P

SCRIPTURE

OBSERVATION

APPLICATION

PRAYER

FEBRUARY 21
DAY 52 OF 365

DEVOTIONAL

Exodus 29-30 shows priests consecrated for service and incense rising before God. Holiness was central to Israel's identity, setting them apart as a people belonging to the Lord and reminding them that worship touched every part of life.

In Mark 6:7-29, Jesus sends out His disciples with authority, even as John the Baptist suffers for truth. Holiness is no longer limited to a priestly line—it flows through every follower who trusts and obeys, even when obedience is costly. Their mission was to embody God's presence wherever they went, pointing others back to Him.

Proverbs 5:15-23 calls for faithfulness in covenant relationships, showing that belief is lived out in ordinary choices. Holiness is not separation from life but faithfulness within it, where every act becomes worship and every choice reflects trust in God.

Today, ask the Spirit to set your life apart in word and deed, reflecting God's holiness in the everyday.

TODAY'S READINGS

EXODUS 29   EXODUS 30
MARK 6:7-29   PROVERBS 5:15-23

S.O.A.P

SCRIPTURE

OBSERVATION

APPLICATION

PRAYER

FEBRUARY 22
DAY 53 OF 365

DEVOTIONAL

Exodus 31-32 records Israel's rebellion with the golden calf, followed by God's grief over their sin. By Exodus 33:1-6, the people mourn as they realize that without His presence, they are lost. Even in failure, Moses intercedes, reminding us that God's presence is the only hope for His people.

In Mark 6:30-56, Jesus multiplies bread, walks on water, and heals the sick. Where Israel doubted, Christ shows that God's presence is near, abundant, and faithful. Wilderness moments can still become places of provision and wonder because His presence never leaves us.

Psalm 25:1-7 lifts a plea for forgiveness and guidance. True belief trusts not in our perfection but in God's mercy to lead us forward, knowing His presence goes before and behind us.

Today, invite the Spirit to remind you that God's presence is with you, even when you stumble.

TODAY'S READINGS

EXODUS 31 EXODUS 32
EXODUS 33:1-6 MARK 6:30-56 PSALM 25:1-7

S.O.A.P

SCRIPTURE

OBSERVATION

APPLICATION

PRAYER

FEBRUARY 23

DAY 54 OF 365

DEVOTIONAL

Exodus 33:7-23 and 34 recount Moses asking to see God's glory. The Lord reveals His goodness, proclaiming His compassion and mercy. This glimpse of God's glory changed Moses, and every encounter with His presence still transforms us today.

Mark 7:1-30 shows Jesus exposing empty traditions and lifting up genuine faith—even from outsiders. Just as God's glory was not confined to a tent, Christ reveals His glory wherever hearts trust Him. The Spirit makes that glory shine even in ordinary lives.

Psalm 25:8-15 reminds us that the Lord instructs the humble in His ways. Belief is not about knowing everything but being willing to be changed by the One who shows Himself to us, and His glory softens our hearts to follow.

Today, ask the Spirit to reveal God's glory in Christ, shaping your life in His presence.

TODAY'S READINGS

EXODUS 33:7-23   EXODUS 34
MARK 7:1-30   PSALM 25:8-15

S.O.A.P

SCRIPTURE

OBSERVATION

APPLICATION

PRAYER

FEBRUARY 24
DAY 55 OF 365

DEVOTIONAL

Exodus 35-36 shows Israel bringing offerings so generously that more than enough was collected for the tabernacle. God's work was supplied not by force but by willing hearts that overflowed with gratitude. Their generosity became a testimony to His abundance and a reminder that when God stirs His people, His purposes will never lack provision.

In Mark 7:31-37 and 8:1-13, Jesus opens ears, loosens tongues, and feeds multitudes. His abundance is not measured by human limits but by heaven's resources. What His people offered in faith, He multiplied in power.

Psalm 25:16-22 cries for deliverance and mercy. The same God who hears our prayers also provides for our needs, surrounding us with grace that is never exhausted and mercy that never runs dry.

Today, trust the Spirit to multiply what you place in God's hands, turning little into more than enough.

TODAY'S READINGS

EXODUS 35   EXODUS 36

MARK 7:31-37   MARK 8:1-13   PSALM 25:16-22

S.O.A.P

SCRIPTURE

OBSERVATION

APPLICATION

PRAYER

FEBRUARY 25
DAY 56 OF 365

DEVOTIONAL

Exodus 37-38 shows skilled workers building the tabernacle exactly as God commanded. Their faithfulness in detail reflected a trust that every instruction mattered, even when the reason was not clear. Ordinary obedience became holy worship, turning craftsmanship into an act of devotion.

In Mark 8:14-38 and 9:1, the disciples struggle to grasp Jesus's teaching, yet He calls them to take up their cross and follow Him. Faith often requires stepping forward without seeing the whole picture. Belief is not built on perfect understanding but on trusting the One who leads us into life, even when the path looks costly.

Proverbs 6:1-11 warns against laziness, urging diligence and wisdom. Belief shows itself in steady obedience, not empty words, and God honors even the smallest step of faith when it is offered to Him.

Today, ask the Spirit for courage to obey even when you don't yet understand the outcome.

TODAY'S READINGS

EXODUS 37   EXODUS 38
MARK 8:14-38   MARK 9:1   PROVERBS 6:1-11

S.O.A.P

SCRIPTURE

OBSERVATION

APPLICATION

PRAYER

FEBRUARY 26
DAY 57 OF 365

DEVOTIONAL

Exodus 39-40 celebrates the completion of the tabernacle, and the glory of the Lord fills it so powerfully that even Moses cannot enter. God's promise was never just about design—it was always about His presence dwelling with His people. His glory turned their work into worship, showing that what is offered in obedience becomes holy in His hands.

In Mark 9:2-32, Jesus is transfigured before His disciples, revealing His glory and pointing to the resurrection. Just as the cloud filled the tabernacle, God's glory shines fully in Christ, and the Spirit now makes His dwelling in us.

Psalm 26 rejoices in walking before the Lord with integrity. Belief anchors us in His presence, where His glory fills not only buildings but also hearts yielded to Him and made holy by His Spirit, shaping the way we live each day.

Today, invite the Spirit to fill every part of your life with the glory of Christ.

TODAY'S READINGS

EXODUS 39   EXODUS 40
MARK 9:2-32   PSALM 26:1-12

S.O.A.P

SCRIPTURE

OBSERVATION

APPLICATION

PRAYER

FEBRUARY 27
DAY 58 OF 365

DEVOTIONAL

Leviticus 1-3 outlines the sacrifices that allowed Israel to draw near to God. Every act of worship was a step closer to His presence, even for a broken people who needed constant reminders of His grace.

In Mark 9:33-50 and 10:1-12, Jesus teaches humility, warns against sin, and calls His followers to covenant faithfulness. The sacrifices foreshadowed this life—one where drawing near to God shapes how we live with one another in love and obedience. His presence is no longer confined to rituals but revealed in transformed hearts.

Psalm 27:1-6 proclaims, "The Lord is my light and my salvation—whom shall I fear?" Belief is fearless trust in the God who draws near, turning fear into confidence and weakness into strength because His nearness is our good.

Today, ask the Spirit to draw you close to Christ, where fear is cast out by His perfect love.

TODAY'S READINGS

EVITICUS 1   LEVITICUS 2   LEVITICUS 3
MARK 9:33-50   MARK 10:1-12   PSALM 27:1-6

S.O.A.P

SCRIPTURE

OBSERVATION

APPLICATION

PRAYER

FEBRUARY 28
DAY 59 OF 365

DEVOTIONAL

Leviticus 4-5:13 provides instructions for sin offerings, showing that God made provision for forgiveness even when His people fell short. Mercy was built into the covenant because He knew their weakness—and ours. His mercy was always greater than their sin.

In Mark 10:13-31, Jesus welcomes children and challenges the rich, teaching that the kingdom belongs to the humble who come with empty hands. Mercy is never earned; it is received by faith because God gives what we could never gain on our own. His call to follow is both costly and life-giving.

Psalm 27:7-14 cries, "Teach me your way, Lord." Belief waits with courage, confident that His mercy covers every failure and keeps us in His love until the end.

Today, let the Spirit remind you that God's mercy is greater than your weakness and strong enough to carry you forward.

TODAY'S READINGS

LEVITICUS 4   LEVITICUS 5:1-13
MARK 10:13-31   PSALM 27:7-14

S.O.A.P

SCRIPTURE

OBSERVATION

APPLICATION

PRAYER

www.ingramcontent.com/pod-product-compliance
Lightning Source LLC
Chambersburg PA
CBHW070207100426
42743CB00013B/3087